Lost and found

Story written by Alison Hawes
Illustrated by Tim Archbold

Speed Sounds

Consonants

Ask your child to say the sounds (not the letter names) clearly and quickly, in and out of order. Make sure he or she does not add 'uh' to the end of the sounds, e.g. 'f' not 'fuh'.

Each box contains one sound. Focus sounds for this story are circled.

f	l	m	n	r	s	v	z	sh	th	ng
ff	ll	mm	nn	rr	ss	ve	zz			nk
ph	le	mb	**kn**	wr	**se**		se			
			gn		c		s			
					ce					

b	c	d	g	h	j	p	qu	t	w	x	y	ch
bb	k	dd	gg		g	pp		tt	wh			tch
	ck		gu		ge							
					dge							

Vowels

Ask your child to say the sounds in and out of order.

a	e ea	i	o	u	ay	ee y	igh i	ow o
at	h**e**n	**i**n	**o**n	**u**p	d**ay**	s**ee**	h**igh**	bl**ow**

oo	oo	ar	or oor ore	air	ir	ou	oy oi
z**oo**	l**oo**k	c**ar**	f**or**	f**air**	wh**ir**l	sh**ou**t	b**oy**

Story Green Words

For each word ask your child to read the separate sounds, e.g. 'b-u-s', 'p-oo-l' and then blend sounds together to make the word, e.g. 'bus', 'pool'. Sometimes one sound is represented by more than one letter, e.g. 'th', 'oo'. These are underlined.

snout down toy stalls*

Ask your child to say the syllables and then read the whole word.

single fairground roundabout office

Ask your child to read the root first and then the whole word with the suffix.

shout → shouted bounce → bounced nod → nodded

sudden → suddenly dribble → dribbled can → cans

proud → proudly disappoint → disappointed

* Challenge Words

Vocabulary Check

Tell your child the meaning of each word in the context of the story.

	definition:	**sentence:**
snout	*an animal's long nose*	*The mouse had a green scarf and a long, thin snout.*
nodded off	*fell asleep*	*She nodded off on the bus back to her house.*
lost and found office	*a place where lost things are kept at a bus station*	*Dad took Jess to the Lost and Found office.*
delighted	*very happy about something*	*Jess was delighted.*

Red Words

Red words don't sound like they look. Ask your child to read the words but if he or she gets stuck read the word to your child.

brother	anyone	over	was
would	water	all	could
her	two	does	want
said	baby	they	brother
over	ball	go	other

Lost and found

Do not read the story to your child first. Point to the words as your child reads. If your child gets stuck on a word help him or her say the sounds and blend them together. Re-read each sentence to your child to help him or her remember what he or she has read. Discuss what is happening on each page.

Dad and Jess had a fun day out at the fairground.

They went round and round on the roundabout. They went round and round on the big wheel and looked at the stalls. “Let’s see if we can win a cuddly toy,” Dad said.

Jess had a go on the last stall. She was lucky and knocked down a stack of cans – with a single sand bag!

"Good throw! You can choose a toy," said the man.
"Thank you, can I have the cuddly mouse?" asked Jess.

The mouse had a green scarf and a long, thin snout.

"I'm going to give this mouse to Jack," said Jess.
(Jack was Jess's little brother.)

It had been a long, fun day and Jess was worn out. She nodded off on the bus back to her house.

"Quick!" Dad shouted. "Get up, Jess, or we'll miss our stop!"

As the bus left, Jess suddenly stopped. "Oh no!" she said. "I've left the mouse on the bus!"

Dad and Jess followed the bus and ran all the way up to the roundabout.

"Stop!" they shouted loudly, but the bus did not stop.

The next day, Dad took Jess to the Lost and Found office.

Jess asked about the mouse. “Has he been found?”
“Sorry, no,” said the man.

Jess was very disappointed.
She had wanted Jack
to have the mouse.

On the way out, a girl stopped Jess.

"Does your mouse have a green scarf round his neck?" she asked.

"Yes!" said Jess.

"Then this must be your mouse," said the girl. "I found him on the bus."

Jess was delighted.
"Thank you very much!" she said.
"He's for my baby brother."

At her house, Jess proudly handed the mouse to Jack.

"Look! This is for you, Jack. It's a mouse," she said.

Jack bounced the mouse on his knee.

"Mou-Mou!" he dribbled.

"Mou-Mou!" Jess giggled.

Now ask your child to re-read the story helping him or her think about the best way to read each sentence.

Questions to talk about

Read the questions aloud to your child and ask him or her to find the answers on the relevant pages. Do not ask your child to read the questions – the words are harder than he or she can read at the moment.

pp.9–10	How did Jess win the toy mouse?
p.10	Why did Jess want to give the mouse to Jack?
p.11	Which line tells us that Dad woke Jess up suddenly?
p.12	Jess left the mouse on the bus. How did she feel?
p.13	What happened at the Lost and Found office?
p.14	How did the girl know that the mouse belonged to Jess?
p.15	How was Jess feeling at the end of the story?

Questions to read and answer

Ask your child to read the questions and find the correct answer in the story.

1. Dad and Jess went to the **fairground / park / zoo**.

2. The mouse had a **short, thin / long, thin / large, thin** snout.

3. Dad and Jess went to the **Lost and Found office / roundabout / shop**.

4. The girl found the mouse **at the fairground / in a park / on the bus**.

5. Jess handed the mouse to her **gran / brother / dad**.

Speedy Green Words

Ask your child to read the words clearly and quickly – across the rows, down the columns, and in and out of order.

out	girl	must	fair
green	day	about	took
house	look	very	scarf
wheel	way	mouse	our
loud	knee	day	round